275

Gaddy

(62-18624)

3-19-63
11-11-63

Books by Walter Lippmann

Western Unity and
the Common Market

Western Unity and the Common Market

by
WALTER LIPPMANN

An Atlantic Monthly Press Book
BOSTON · Little, Brown and Company · TORONTO

ATLANTIC—LITTLE, BROWN BOOKS
ARE PUBLISHED BY
LITTLE, BROWN AND COMPANY
IN ASSOCIATION WITH
THE ATLANTIC MONTHLY PRESS

*Published simultaneously in Canada
by Little, Brown & Company (Canada) Limited*

PRINTED IN THE UNITED STATES OF AMERICA

to
Jean Monnet

Editor's Note

During the past winter the United States became interested in a grand design which called for the enlargement of the European Common Market to include Great Britain, and, following that, a partnership between the United States and this enlarged Common Market in a low-tariff trading area.

Mr. Lippmann went abroad in April to visit the Continental capitals and London and on his return wrote the following articles. They were the first to arouse American readers to an awareness of the deep rivalries within the Western world.

EDWARD WEEKS

Contents

I. Rivalry in the West

RECENTLY I went to Western Europe in order to have a look at the grand project of the Western Alliance — the Common Market, enlarged by the admission of Great Britain and joined with us in a wide free trading area. I set out with a strong conviction that the project was desirable, indeed necessary, that it was part of the manifest destiny of the Western world.

I still think this. But I confess that my enthusiasm was stronger than my knowledge of what are the dominant forces in the new Europe as it has come to be recently. I had not realized that the grand project was complicated by the nuclear stalemate, by the success of the Common Market, by the lack of any known and clear succession in France and Germany, and by our own fading economic pre-eminence.

The road ahead will be a rough one, and if the hopes of the Western Alliance are to be realized, it will not be soon. The grand project is caught up in a crisis of power and leadership within the Western Alliance. We have a right to believe that with patience, lucidity and resolution the crisis will eventually be overcome. For it is true, I think, that throughout Europe there is a deep and ardent determination to conquer the obstacles, if necessary by outliving them.

When I went abroad I had braced myself for heavy doses of briefing on what is surely a dull exercise for a journalist, namely, the commercial problems of the Common Market, of Britain and the Commonwealth and of the European neutrals. I soon learned that, important as the commercial issues are, the critical issue within the alliance comes from a rebellion against the American monopoly of nuclear power.

There are exceedingly difficult economic issues between Great Britain and the European community. But in the eyes of General de Gaulle, who leads the rebellion, the unacceptable fact about Great Britain is its "special relation" with the United States. That special relation does not mean merely that the " Anglo-Saxons," as General de Gaulle calls Britain and America, speak English and quickly call each other by their first names. Specifically, the unacceptable special relation is that Britain has access to our nuclear monopoly while France is denied access.

M. Raymond Aron, for example, writing in *Le Figaro*, says it is hard to see why it is safe for nuclear knowledge to cross the Atlantic to England and not to cross the English Channel to France. For General de Gaulle this special relation in nuclear affairs would make Britain an agent of the United States within the European community. Not only would Britain have an especially strong position, but also it would have knowledge which prevented it from speaking freely within the community. There would be questions which could not be discussed fully and frankly in the community because Britain would have special knowledge which she could not convey to her fellow members. So it would be a wonder indeed if for this reason alone General de Gaulle did not seek a way to prevent Britain from entering the European community.

I did my best to understand exactly the nature of the French rebellion against our nuclear monopoly. I do not doubt that pride, prestige, status, and all that sort of thing are involved in it. But they do not fully explain it. What I am about to report is my own personal conclusion, although it is based on some first-hand inquiries.

In all of Western Europe, and particularly in France — the most articulate in this field — there is a conviction which does not exist equally in this country: that it is an accomplished fact that there is a balance of power with the Soviet Union. Quite generally, the Europeans believe that the East-West political stalemate which results from the nuclear deadlock is not soon going to be broken, and that therefore while there will be no nuclear war, and no small conventional wars about Berlin and Germany, nothing constructive and large can be negotiated either.

Where we differ from the Continentals is not that we expect great things to be negotiated, but that they treat the nuclear stalemate as an accomplished fact, while we are continually concerned with how much it costs in sweat and worry to accomplish it and to keep it accomplished.

Thus, for example, General de Gaulle and Dr. Adenauer take a "harder" line about Berlin than we do. This is not because they are more ready than we are to go to war about Berlin. It is because they look on war, given the nuclear stalemate, as inconceivable. We do not regard it as inconceivable. Thus we mobilized when Berlin was divided by the wall. The French and Germans did not. It is rubbish, therefore, to write about this kind of thing as if it were an argument between the legendary old heroes and the soft young men. Seen from Washington, where the button would have to be pressed, it is not so altogether certain that the nuclear stalemate is an unequivocally accomplished fact.

The rebellion against the American monopoly is taking place within the context of the American capacity to prevent a nuclear war. The so-called independent nuclear force is often talked about as if it were a conceivable alternative to the American capacity. It is not in any sense an alternative. General de Gaulle says that by the end of 1963 France will have a *force de frappe*, that is to say a nuclear striking force, capable of killing twenty million people. That is something in the way of force but it is no match for, and is no independent defense against, the Soviet Union.

The question is: What is it? I think I am right in saying that the French striking force is to be a French national force. When would it be used? When France is attacked. What would constitute an attack on France? A blockade of Berlin? No. France would be attacked when her real frontier, which is the Rhine River, is violated. Would the nuclear weapon be used if the violation of the Rhine were done with conventional weapons? Yes. But would not France be demolished if it made the first nuclear strike? No, for Russia would be deterred by the United States.

In what sense, then, we may ask ourselves, would

the *force de frappe* be an independent deterrent? From inquiries I made previously, as well as this year, I take the answer to be twofold. First, if France has the capability of killing twenty million Russians, it might have the power to resist becoming involved in a nuclear war which broke out, say, in Asia, beyond the limits of French national interests. And second, if France can make the first nuclear strike, one which compelled the United States to join her, the ultimate decision of nuclear war or peace is no longer in Washington.

The independent French national striking force is the current substitute for the stationing of American troops on the frontier of the Cold War. They were put there ten years or more ago to act as the "plate-glass window" or the "trip wire" in case the Russians marched to the West. If those American troops were attacked, there would be no debate in Washington, as there was in the two World Wars, about going to war in Europe. The *force de frappe* is a device to engage the United States so that the initiative in nuclear strategy would be mainly in Continental Europe.

I hope no one will regard this as the exposure of a wicked plot. It is not a wicked plot. But it is power politics as played by the masters of the game and we must not be pharisaical about it. We do not have a divine right to have in our own hands, rather than in European hands, the ultimate decisions. But it is in our interest to hold on to the ultimate decisions, if we can, and we must not be beguiled and bemused by any sentimental adulation of venerable statesmen who are not moved by sentimentality. In other words, we shall have to play the game and be resourceful enough to protect our ultimate interest and to promote our bigger hopes.

II. Britain and the Common Market

We must bear it in mind that while the Common Market, as established by the Treaty of Rome in 1957, deals only with economic relations, it has been agreed by all six members that they will soon sign another treaty, which is now being negotiated, to establish a political unity. Their object is to create a new great power which is to be known not as France or Germany but as "Europe." It is in the formation of this new political entity that the issues of the British-American nuclear connection arise.

All of this is not, however, the subject of the formal negotiations which are taking place in Brussels.* They are concerned, we may say, with whether and how Britain can be admitted to the Common Market. They are not avowedly concerned with British membership in the new political entity which has still to be created. Nevertheless, the political and strategic

* This goes to press in June, 1962.

[13]

issues are, I feel sure, controlling, at least in France, and how they are to be resolved no one now knows.

We can be sure that, unresolved, these problems will not make it easier to solve the economic issues, which in themselves are very difficult indeed. To understand the nature of the economic difficulty, around which the Brussels negotiations revolve, we must realize what is the basic compact of the Common Market.

It is a bargain between French agriculture and German industry. The key to this bargain is that French agriculture is being modernized and is becoming increasingly productive. At bottom the Common Market enables France to sell the bulk of the basic food — wheat and meat — protected against Canada, Australia, New Zealand, the Argentine and the United States by a common variable levy which would prevent imports, no matter how low in price, from competing in the European market. In return, German industry primarily, but also Italian, Belgian and Dutch, have the privilege of free trade within the market and protection against the rest of the world by a customs union.

(I might say that the reciprocal relation between French agriculture and German industry is comparable to the economy of our own political union. The United States is a common market in which there is an economic compact between the industrial Northeast and the agricultural South and West. On a smaller scale, of course, the Common Market in Europe rests on a similar system of reciprocal advantage.)

Now we can see why the British application to join the Common Market raises such difficult questions on both sides of the negotiating table. For Britain buys most of her essential food outside of Europe. The food comes into Britain at the low world price and there is no significant tariff imposed upon it. As a result, the British people enjoy the advantage of cheaper food than do the Continental people. The French pay their farmers $2.25 a bushel for wheat which brings only $1.60 on the British market. Thus, in Britain wheat flour costs at retail about 18 cents per kilogram ($2\frac{1}{5}$ pounds); in France, Germany and Italy the wheat flour costs about 21 cents. Beef costs the British at retail about $1.66 a kilogram; it costs the French and Italians about $2.16.

The biggest economic issue in the negotiations arises from the fact that France and what might be called the fundamentalists of the Common Market in Brussels, Bonn and Rome, say that to be admitted, Britain must open her market to French agriculture and in effect close it to Australia and New Zealand, North and South America. Britain must impose, probably after a transitional period of about seven years, the common agricultural tariff of the Common Market. If Britain does not do this, she may be excluded, and then her industrial exports must face the common industrial tariff of the Common Market.

This poses a very hard choice both in Paris and in London. How much the French will wish to sharpen the issue depends, as I have been saying, on great political and strategic questions. But there are powerful economic interests in France which, leaving all political considerations aside, will press for very hard terms. France is in the midst of the same kind of agricultural revolution which has created our own farm problem. For example, the yield of wheat per acre has increased by more than half over the prewar levels. France not only is able to feed her people, but also she has surpluses to export. In the years from 1950 to 1960 France exported about one-eighth of her total wheat production of 32 million tons. About a third of that total export went to Germany.

The French farmers, like our own, are a powerful political force. They are interested in exports at high prices, and Britain seems a natural market for French agriculture. French and other Continental industrialists view higher food prices for British workers as a wage-equalizing factor. It would therefore be most difficult for any French government to allow Britain to enjoy cheap food from overseas, thus excluding French exports to Britain, and at the same time to enjoy a free run of the big common industrial market.

For the British the terms for admission present a truly agonizing decision. If the British must shut out the old dominions, which are the producers of temperate agricultural products such as wheat and meat and butter, the old political and human allegiance of the Empire and the Commonwealth will suffer a rude and painful, if not a fatal, shock. The issue is deep, momentous, and highly charged with sentiment. No solution of it is in sight at this writing. To find a solution, the Continentals will have to move into a much more generous and flexible position than General de Gaulle and Dr. Adenauer now occupy. The British are not so hard pressed that they can be brought to a kind of unconditional surrender to Paris and Bonn. Thus the immediate fate of the grand project depends primarily on Paris and Bonn.

I know that this sounds gloomy. For the short run the prospect is gloomy if we expect a full solution in which Britain "joins" the European Community of General de Gaulle and Dr. Adenauer. This is so difficult that we may count ourselves fortunate if the negotiations are not broken off and if a way is found to continue them, perhaps for some years. For in the long run, the grand project will, I believe, be realized. There is a very large popular momentum behind it, based on the manifest economic advantages of union and on the great hopes of peace and security which go with union. For ourselves, we shall be dealing with the bigger realities if we keep our hopes and our policies bound up with the will to get on with and to achieve the grand project. For the Europe of 1962 is not the permanent and final shape of Europe. It could change in a few months.

III. De Gaulle's Europe

AT HIS press conference on Tuesday, May 15, 1962, General de Gaulle made it quite clear that in his mind "Europe" should be organized and led by a Franco-German combination. The General does not regard Britain, which he describes as an "island," as genuinely European, and he thinks of the United States, though its presence is still necessary for defense, as destined eventually to withdraw from Europe and in the near future to exercise a receding influence in European affairs. The true Europe is to be led by the Franco-Germans and not by the Anglo-Saxons. It is to make itself sufficiently powerful to come to terms with the Soviet Union and thus to have "Europe" extend from the Atlantic to the Urals.

This is a formidable conception of policy. For the core of it, the Franco-German combination, has real substance. In spite of their many wars there is a historical connection between France and the western part of Germany which goes back to the Roman Empire. Economically, the two countries are complementary; and in the Common Market they are creating an economy which is so rich and so dynamic that already it has a bargaining power in the world which, as we shall see in the proposed tariff negotiations, is superior to that of Britain and the Commonwealth and at least equal to that of the United States. There are also deep but mixed bonds of memory and of emotion which unite the two peoples in the belief that war, which for both of them was a tragedy and a humiliation, must never again come between them.

There is, too, the belief that while separately they are only medium-sized powers, combined they will be the core of a new great world power. In that connection we must remind ourselves that although Germany is solemnly pledged by treaty not to make nuclear weapons, the European nuclear striking force which General de Gaulle wants so much, could be created much more quickly by Franco-German co-operation.

Yet there is another side to the picture. The Franco-German combination today is an alliance between General de Gaulle and Dr. Adenauer. That is enough to warn us not to regard the Gaullist conception of Europe as an accomplished fact. For in both France and in West Germany there is a monarch but there is no crown prince. The two old kings have not prepared and cannot control the future, and so in our own calculations of policy we cannot treat as the shape of the Europe to come what the old kings now say about it.

I shall not attempt here to say, because I do not know, what will happen in France when General de Gaulle departs. The basic institutions of France are still all there, and France is in fact, as one Frenchman put it to me, a liberal state ruled by a self-determining king. We have a right to believe that the French administration and local government will go on in spite of the disloyalty which is so widespread. But General de Gaulle has dismantled representative government in France, replacing it with his own personal rule nourished by popular plebiscite. Since France is not a hereditary monarchy, those who are concerned with such things are saying — not very loudly at present — that they do not see how representative government is to be restored and a stable succession to General de Gaulle arranged.

Nevertheless, we must not make too much of the political instability of France. It is an old nation; and, with all the dreams of grandeur, it is a completed and territorially satisfied nation. It has a highly educated population and its economy is flourishing.

But the instability of Germany has profounder consequences. The retirement of Dr. Adenauer cannot be far off. Under his iron leadership the West Germans have followed his foreign policy, but it is most improbable that there is any successor to Adenauer whom the parties and the factions will follow in the same way. The Franco-German combination, which is the keystone of General de Gaulle's policy, will no doubt remain. But I find it hard to think from what I learned in Berlin and Bonn that the existing policy will be followed with the same discipline, the same inflexibility, and the same dogmatism.

I say this because I am persuaded that West Germany, which is defeated, divided from the rest of Germany, and is still haunted by the memories of Nazism, has not yet achieved the kind of sovereignty, the kind of self-confidence and self-assurance, which will enable it to make its own national policy. West Germany has made a brilliant economic recovery. But in world politics it is not as yet a principal power. It is the object of the diplomacy of the other powers, and its inner life is pushed and pulled from the outside. All of Germany is the object of the great conflict between the Soviet Union and the Atlantic Alliance. West Germany itself is the object of the conflict within the Atlantic Alliance as to who shall lead the West in world affairs.

De Gaulle's Europe

Dr. Adenauer is much aware that these conflicting external pressures work within Germany, and because of them he is insecure and feels that the least risk is to be inflexible and to stand pat. The "hard line," which is so much General de Gaulle's specialty these days, is designed primarily to keep the Germans from straying away from the Franco-German combination, to keep them from working with the Americans and the British to find an accommodation about Berlin, or even, as is always a possibility for the Germans, of going along with Dr. Kroll toward a larger Russo-German deal.

We cannot pretend, and we should not try to pretend, that we believe in or would welcome a Franco-German "Europe." We shall not be alone in refusing to applaud it and in promoting a wider community. Opposed to the exclusive and restrictive Europe of General de Gaulle and Dr. Adenauer there is a liberal party within the whole area of the Common Market. Its leaders are Jean Monnet himself; M. Spaak, the Foreign Minister of Belgium; the Netherlands government; Dr. Hallstein, chairman of the Commission of the European Economic Community and, I should say, the leading spirits of the present Italian coalition. In Germany there belong to this party men like Dr. Erhard, who may be Dr. Adenauer's successor; the leading big German industrialists; the Free Democrats on the right and the Social Democrats on the left.

Some of them want a more highly federated Europe than they are likely to get. It is to them that General de Gaulle was referring when he spoke of "Utopian construction." A federated Europe may well be a Utopian idea, but what matters practically is that the men and groups I have named are all of them favorable to British membership and adamant in their support of the Atlantic Alliance.

IV. The German Interest

THE VISION of a Gaullist Europe — the Western Continent led by France with the English-speaking nations on the outside — would be wholly unrealizable without the permanent support of West Germany. So far as the vision is credible at all it is so because of the relationship between General de Gaulle and Dr. Adenauer and the success of the Common Market.

For myself, I think that a Franco-German Europe under French leadership is an optical illusion which will pass away with the two venerable figures who have created it. For a closed, Continental Franco-German community is contrary to the vital national, political, military and economic interests of the German Federal Republic. The vital interests of the German nation as a whole are bound up with the wider association of which the Atlantic nations are the core.

I do not think that the fundamental issue will be determined by, or be much affected by, the personalities and the frictions of diplomatic intercourse. General de Gaulle is a towering figure who plays the game of international politics as it was taught by Machiavelli and played in other days by men like Richelieu and Talleyrand. He knows that we are not at odds with him over a trivial misunderstanding due to tactlessness and bad manners. We are at odds with him because in fact his ambition to take the leadership of Europe is irreconcilable with our vital need to retain the ultimate power in nuclear affairs. We must have that power because we have the ultimate responsibility.

General de Gaulle is playing for very grand stakes and he will respect us most if we play it that way too. He will not be moved by blandishments, bribes or threats but only by moves which affect the balance of forces in the game he has chosen to play.

Those moves will come from Germany. If the Germans turn inwardly to a Gaullist Europe, they may conceivably — just barely conceivably — be able at great cost and at great risk to make it a going concern. In doing this they will be delivering a fearful blow at the Atlantic Community and at NATO which is their defense. If, on the other hand, the Germans turn outwardly, which would mean to insist on viable terms for Britain and the Commonwealth, Gaullist Europe will be nothing more than an idle dream.

This momentous German decision does not depend

on the personal feelings of Dr. Adenauer and on how assiduously he is adulated from Washington. So far as we are concerned, our appeal to the Germans must not be to their vanity or to their pride but to their common sense. Dr. Adenauer, we must remember, is now a very old man; and with the end of his regime so near, the struggle for the succession has begun. His power to commit Germany for the future is about like that of an American President in the last few months of his term.

There is no reason to think that the Adenauer–de Gaulle axis against the Anglo-Saxons will be the center of the policy of Dr. Adenauer's successors. Already Dr. Schroeder, the Foreign Minister, has announced that Germany would press for the admission of Britain.

A Franco-German axis is contrary to German interests. In the first place, it jeopardizes dangerously the United States military commitment on the continent of Europe. After Dr. Adenauer realized what his first angry interview in Berlin had done, and when he had read General de Gaulle's recent press conference, he said in another interview, "We must under no circumstances release the United States from the defense community. Without the United States we are lost."

In the second place, the Germans will realize that a Gaullist Europe assumes the continuing partition of Germany. A Gaullist Europe will oppose any opening to the East which in the course of time might bring about the reunification of Germany. The hard line that France takes about Berlin and the Soviet Union is founded, we must be sure to understand, on a basic French national determination not to have to live with a large reunited Germany. At bottom the hard policy is directed not against the Russians but against those Germans who want to make an opening to the East. Its purpose is to make any departure from the present position seem un-German and unpatriotic.

Germany's real interests cannot include Gaullist grandeur. Germany's real interests run with the Atlantic Community and with a wider European society, open enough to be an attraction to the European peoples on the other side of the Iron Curtain. To promote this wider community is the way to save Berlin, it is the way to reunite Germany, it is the way to unite Europe, it is the way to confront peaceably and successfully the Soviet Union.

V.   America, and Europe's Defense

ONE OF THE main reasons why our relations with General de Gaulle are seriously disturbed is that the Kennedy administration has decided not to alter the established policy, which is not to share with France, as we do with Great Britain, the know-how and the facilities of nuclear power. At first glance the cure for the trouble would seem to be to invite the French into the Anglo-American nuclear club.

But the problem becomes more complicated when we realize, as the British now do, that although they have a considerable nuclear power of their own, always assuming the over-all protection of the United States, it is a power which is on the way to becoming obsolete. Because it is impossibly expensive, the British have already retired from the race in missiles, and they know that when the bombers become obsolete, say within the next ten years, Britain will cease to be a nuclear power in its own right.

Thus our "special relation" in nuclear affairs is destined to disappear within a period of time. The time will not be much longer than it would take France, which is now far behind Britain, to make itself as strong in nuclear power as Britain is today.

That Britain has already retired from the missile race and that it realizes that it has an obsolescent nuclear power prove that the whole British effort was a mistake in the first place. We allowed ourselves to be persuaded to support the mistake by an amendment to the McMahon Act. The question today is whether to make compensation to France for that mistake, which time is curing anyway, by repeating the same mistake with France.

After much debate and soul-searching, the Administration decided, I think rightly, that the original principle of the McMahon Act is sound, that within the Western Alliance the ultimate responsibility in nuclear affairs must be in one capital, not in two or three. For the United States the predicament would be intolerable if the key to the use of our strategic nuclear forces were not in Washington.

We have this power because we had to build it. Our nuclear power is, as a matter of fact, the core of the defense of Europe and of the West. We cannot allow this power to be set in motion by others. We must keep the ultimate right to decide whether and when it shall be used. A weak and independent nuclear force within the Western Alliance, a force which could start a world war but could not finish it, would be a danger to the peace of the world and to our own national security.

Not for a moment do I believe that the British would dream of committing a gross betrayal of the United States, which would be to buy admission to the Common Market by offering to France the nuclear know-how acquired from us. Nor do I share the view that the British have no other card, except betrayal of the United States, to play against General de Gaulle.

There is a very strong card, which is at once British and American, in what has been called the grand project. This looks to the admission of Britain and some other European states to the Common Market, to an association with it of the European neutrals, to a friendly accommodation with the Commonwealth, and, with all this, partnership of the United States in a great open and low-tariff trading area.

It must be understood in France and in Germany, as I believe it is in Belgium, the Netherlands and Italy, that the grand project is not a Utopian contraption, nor is it an insidious American attempt to control Europe. It is based on the hard condition of the postwar world. The United States needs this large liberal trading area if it is to expand its trade and thus be able to earn the hard money to finance its military and civilian commitments overseas. For this reason, if Paris and Bonn wreck the grand project, there is almost certain to follow a severe retrenchment in our dollar commitments overseas.

There should be no illusions about this, particularly in Bonn. If the European Economic Community becomes a closed, restrictive and exclusive society, the United States will not be able to earn the costs of defending that community on the ground in Europe. The United States will be compelled to insist that the defense of this restricted Europe be paid for by the restricted Europe. With our dollar deficit what it is, with our mounting obligations in this hemisphere and in Asia, we shall not be able to go on subsidizing the local and tactical defense of the European continent.

We must see to it that this is understood in the places where the final decisions will be taken about the admission of Great Britain and about the partnership with the United States. I am confident that it will be understood.

VI.   The Improvement of the Western Position

In my view, in the past year or so the world balance of forces has become rather more favorable to the Western Community. I know from my newspaper experience how risky it is to be optimistic, and I know that the man who wishes to play it safe will always lean to Cassandra, never to Pollyanna. For if Cassandra is right, which I am sorry to say is all too frequently, the prudent man becomes without any trouble at all a true prophet. If, on the other hand, Cassandra is wrong, everyone is too well pleased to remember what he said.

Nevertheless, in the historic confrontation between international Communism and the Western society our position is, I believe, improved. I could provide plenty of gloom about what lies ahead in South America, in Africa, and perhaps in South Asia. And in regard to the problems of the less developed, emerging nations I make no concessions at all to Pollyanna. But what seems to me to have become better is the relationships of power between the two great centers of power on this planet; and quite briefly, and of course by simplifying much, I shall try to say why I think this is happening.

I shall be so rash as to say that, primarily and fundamentally, the balance of military power is now very considerably in our favor. Indeed, I am told by those whose expertness I most respect that the West, and at the center of it the United States, is now much stronger than the Soviet Union. Unless the Soviet Union achieves a great scientific breakthrough in the next nuclear tests — for example an anti-missile missile or a bomb of decisive size which cannot be repelled — our lead in the race of armaments can be called decisive.

To be sure, we cannot be absolutely certain of this. There may, for example, be undisclosed political weaknesses in the West. Most certainly our military strength is the very last thing to talk about boastfully. I have hesitated a long time whether it is proper to talk about it at all. It would be tempting the gods to boast of it, and in fact it should be talked about only with the greatest reserve and humility. But I am speaking of it because it is now the controlling fact in the world situation, and it must therefore be known to those who form opinions if they are to understand the world situation today.

There is good reason to think that it is well understood in the highest places in Moscow. The best evidence of this is twofold. There is the prudent moderation of Soviet policy in Berlin and Southeast Asia, there is the stubborn refusal of the Soviet Government to sign a treaty to ban nuclear tests. That refusal represents a reversal of Soviet policy, and it is due, I believe, to the realization in Moscow that the Soviet Union is behind in the race of armaments. That is why the Soviets broke the moratorium and that is why they are preparing new tests. Their scientists and generals are hoping for a scientific breakthrough which would change radically and quickly in their favor the balance of power. Our own testing, I should add, is designed to reinsure our present nuclear superiority against the chance of such a Soviet breakthrough.

It is probable that the Soviet Government will not sign a treaty until and unless it has convinced itself that, as so many American scientists believe, no breakthrough which will be decisive in a military sense is likely to be achieved from the atmospheric tests. At this writing the test negotiations are deadlocked. Mr. Khrushchev is listening to Russian scientists who believe that a breakthrough is possible, and Mr. Ken-

[43]

nedy cannot overrule the American scientists who tell him that a Russian breakthrough is not impossible and cannot be ruled out.

In the meantime, there are strong indications that Soviet foreign policy is slowly adjusting itself to the realities of nuclear power. I am thinking particularly about Berlin and about Southeast Asia. The situation in both places has changed in the past year. One might say that in the field of nuclear danger both Berlin and Southeast Asia have to a very considerable degree been de-fused. Neither side is ready to face the risks of pushing the other into a dead-end street from which there is no exit except by a humiliating surrender or a suicidal war. I ascribe this improvement to the success of the President in using our superior strength, which he has helped to reinforce, to promote an accommodating and conciliatory and resourceful diplomacy. Power exercised with restraint and magnanimity is a great persuader in human affairs.

On the plus side for the West, I would put next the brilliant recovery and the growing unity of Western Europe. So rapidly has the standard of living been rising that the Soviet Union no longer has in the Communist and the far left parties, with their constituency among workers, farmers, professionals and intellectuals, strong and reliable instruments of political power inside the Continental countries. The Soviet Union still has influence, of course, but what it has lost is the power to intervene effectively in the internal affairs of Western Europe.

Because of the great growth of wealth since the war, the developments in Italy, for example, are spectacular. Not only has the Italian left split — the Socialists are no longer allied with the Communists in opposing the government, which is liberal and progressive — but in the Communist party itself there is a split between the true believers, the so-called Stalinists, and the younger and more liberally minded men.

One of the most interesting developments in the new and buoyant Western Europe is that the socialist parties in Germany, France, Italy and Great Britain are finding that traditional socialist doctrine has become largely irrelevant. It no longer fits the facts of life. It is a generation out of date. Some of the old socialist doctrine, in particular the welfare state, has been adopted. Much — particularly the public ownership of the means of production — has been bypassed and surpassed by the new European economy which is proving to be highly productive and is creating an affluent European society.

I would name next in my list of favorable developments a by-product of this new European postwar economy. To the less developed nations it is offering a third way to become more productive and to raise their standard of life. They do not have to plunge themselves into a totalitarian system. The new nations do not want to do this. And the alternative is no longer that they should try to imitate vainly our own special American kind of individualistic free enterprise. For the undeveloped and crowded nations it is altogether impossible to duplicate the American economy.

The example of free but planned economy, which comes from the new Europe, is backed by the growing Western accumulation of wealth. This is making it no longer necessary to assume — as perhaps it was necessary even ten years ago — that for the poorer and backward peoples there is only one quick solution to their misery, which is to follow the example of the Soviet Union, which raised itself from poverty and chaos to world power in forty years.

I turn now to the other side, to the more recent developments which are affecting the balance of forces between the two worlds. I have already talked about the balance of military power. Obviously, for the Soviet Union it counsels prudence and a policy not of external expansion but of internal development.

The second point which I would like to note has enormous consequences throughout the world. It is the proven failure of Communist agriculture. The greater part of mankind lives by agriculture, and there is nothing enticing and alluring in the spectacle of the Soviet and Chinese failures. In China the failure is a national disaster. In the Soviet Union the poor yields provide no surpluses for use abroad. This is manifestly a liability for the Soviet position in foreign affairs. Thus it is unable to help China, which is a confession of weakness.

As against the proven agricultural shortages in the Communist world, there are the great surpluses in the non-Communist world. The Western farm problem, which is to dispose of the surpluses, is indeed a hard problem. But, obviously, it is an infinitely easier problem to deal with than the Communist shortages, which can lead — and in China have led — to famine. The contrast between the two agricultural achievements is asserting an enormous influence on the prestige of the two rival societies. For the great majority of the inhabitants of the globe live on the land, and the contrast in agricultural achievements weighs heavily in determining which of the two societies they wish to follow.

Then, there is the Soviet-Chinese conflict. In the longer run it poses what may be the most important threat. For Soviet Russia, the conflict with China may well be so momentous that it could bring about what is known in diplomatic history as a reversal of alliances. Russia's historic expansion is from Europe eastward across Siberia to the Pacific Ocean. Along the path of this expansion the Russians and the Chinese have a common frontier which is about four thousand miles long. Against this frontier the Chinese are pushing north, and they are in imminent collision with the Russians moving east. The Russians, we must remember, have always known — it is bred in their bones — that they cannot become engaged vitally and mortally on their two widely separated frontiers at the same time.

I have been describing the favorable developments, and I hope I have not caused anyone to think that on this estimate of forces we may now expect world events to go just about the way we would like them to go. They will not go that way. In addition to, in a true sense quite independent of, the Western-Soviet conflict, there is a revolutionary condition which prevails in much of Africa and Latin America and South Asia. It has its own native roots and it will not disappear. It will keep these continental areas in turmoil, and it will cause continual friction with the Communist powers. But if, as I have been saying, the basic power relationship is more secure, we should be able to keep Latin

America, Africa and South Asia from becoming the scene of a thermonuclear world war.

Apart from all this, and at the heart of the crucial balance of power between East and West, there is the rivalry within the Atlantic Alliance. I have said that our relations with France and Germany have become difficult. In my view, the underlying explanation for the difficulty is that because it now appears to be possible that the Western position is improving in relation to the Communist world, a rivalry for the leadership of the West has become safer and, therefore, more possible and, therefore, more tempting.

I sometimes think of an analogy from the Second World War. Once the threat to the very existence of Russia and Britain had been overcome, broadly speaking after the Battle of Stalingrad, the rivalries within the anti-Nazi coalition began to come at once to the surface. When the breakout of peace became conceivable, peacetime rivalries reappeared, although there was still a long and bloody war to be fought. Something that is faintly like that is happening with the Atlantic Alliance at this stage of the Cold War.

I was struck, when I was in Europe, with how much it is taken for granted that the United States has created a deterrent to war, how much it is treated as an accomplished fact that we have created the power to prevent the Soviet Union from advancing into Europe.

This accomplished fact, which is a comforting one, has in the eyes of many Europeans a great drawback. It means that the United States is the leading power of the Atlantic Community. It is human, all too human, to think how much more agreeable it would be if the United States were indissolubly committed to the defense of Europe while the questions of when to defend Europe and what to defend it about and how to conduct relations with the outer world were handed over to older and more experienced hands on the European continent.

But this is a grandiose daydream. For the United States cannot, and will not, carry the enormous burden of the alliance and face the catastrophic dangers of a thermonuclear war if, within the alliance, it has lost the initiative and the ultimate responsibility on the issues of peace and war. The President is quite right in telling the French and the Germans that while the United States has no intention of withdrawing from Europe, Europe must realize that the United States could be pushed out of Europe. It could be pushed out if we were maneuvered into a position where we had to defend Europe while the critical decisions that led to war were to be made not in Washington but in Paris or Bonn.

The Improvement of the Western Position

The United States could be pushed out if General de Gaulle and Dr. Adenauer proceed relentlessly with the notion of creating a so-called Europe which excludes Great Britain, which ignores the smaller countries now in the Common Market, which freezes out the neutrals, and which disdains a partnership with the United States.